Contents

The Theory

The Premise of This Guide

Writing is essential to learning. One cannot be educated and yet unable to communicate one's ideas in written form. But, learning to write can occur only through a process of cultivation requiring intellectual discipline. As with any set of complex skills, there are fundamentals of writing that must be internalized and then applied using one's thinking. This guide focuses on the most important of those fundamentals.

Writing for a Purpose

Skilled writers do not write blindly, but purposely. They have an agenda, goal, or objective. Their purpose, together with the nature of what they are writing (and their situation), determines how they write. They write in different ways in different situations for different purposes. There is also a nearly universal purpose for writing, and that is *to say something worth saying about something worth saying something about.*

In general, then, when we write, we translate inner meanings into public words. We put our ideas and experiences into written form. Accurately translating intended meanings into written words is an analytic, evaluative, and creative set of acts. Unfortunately, few people are skilled in this work of translation. Few are able to select and combine words that, so combined, convey an intended meaning to an audience of readers.

Of course, if we are writing for pure pleasure and personal amusement, it may not matter if others do not understand what we write. We may simply enjoy the act of writing itself. This is fine as long as we know that our writing is meant only for us.

Among the various purposes for writing are the following:
- for sheer pleasure
- to express a simple idea
- to convey specific technical information
- to convince the reader to accept an important position or argument
- to challenge the reader to consider a new worldview
- to express what we are learning (or have learned) in a subject

People write in pursuit of many specific and varied agendas. Consider how the purposes would vary for the following writers:

- a media advisor writing political campaign literature
- a newspaper editor deciding how to edit a story to maintain reader interest
- a media consultant writing copy for an advertisement
- a chemist writing a laboratory report
- a novelist writing a novel
- a poet writing a poem
- a student writing a research report

Clearly, one's purpose in writing influences the writing skills one needs and uses. Nevertheless, there are some fundamental writing skills we all need if we are to develop the art of saying something worth saying about something worth saying something about. We call this substantive writing. And learning the art of substantive writing has many important implications for our development as thinkers. For example, it is important in learning how to learn. And, it is important in coming to understand ourselves. It can enable us to gain self-insight, as well as insight into the many dimensions of our lives.

Substantive Writing

To learn how to write something worth reading, we must keep two questions in mind: "Do I have a subject or idea worth writing about?" and "Do I have something of significance to say about it?"

Having recognized possible variations in purpose, we also should recognize that there are core writing tools and skills for writing about anything substantive, for targeting ideas of depth and significance. These tools and skills are the focus of this guide.

The Problem of Impressionistic Writing

The impressionistic mind follows associations, wandering from paragraph to paragraph, drawing no clear distinctions within its thinking and its writing from moment to moment. Being fragmented, it fragments what it writes. Being uncritical, it assumes its own point of view to be insightful and justified, and therefore not in need of justification in comparison to competing points of view. Being self-deceived, it fails to see itself as undisciplined. Being rigid, it does not learn from what it reads, writes, or experiences.

Whatever knowledge the impressionistic mind absorbs is uncritically intermixed with prejudices, biases, myths, and stereotypes. It lacks insight into the importance of understanding how minds create meaning and how reflective minds monitor and evaluate as they write. To discipline our writing, we must go beyond impressionistic thinking.

Writing Reflectively

Unlike the impressionistic mind, the reflective mind seeks meaning, monitors what it writes, draws a clear distinction between its thinking and the thinking of its audience. The reflective mind, being purposeful, adjusts writing to specific goals. Being integrated, it interrelates ideas it is writing with ideas it already commands. Being critical, it assesses what it writes for clarity, accuracy, precision, relevance, depth, breadth, logic, significance, and fairness. Being open to new ways of thinking, it values new ideas and learns from what it writes.

The reflective mind improves its thinking by thinking (reflectively) about it. Likewise, it improves its writing by thinking (reflectively) about writing. It moves back and forth between writing and thinking about how it is writing. It moves forward a bit, and then loops back upon itself to check on its own operations. It checks its tracks. It makes good its ground. It rises above itself and exercises oversight. This applies to the reflective mind while writing — or reading or listening or making decisions.

The foundation for this ability is knowledge of how the mind functions when writing well. For example, if I know (or discover) that what I am writing is difficult for others to understand, I intentionally explain each key sentence more thoroughly and give more examples and illustrations. I look at what I am writing from the readers' point of view.

> The reflective mind creates an inner dialogue with itself, assessing what it is writing while it is writing:
> - Have I stated my main point clearly?
> - Have I explained my main point adequately?
> - Have I given my readers examples from my own experience that connect important ideas to their experience?
> - Have I included metaphors or analogies that illustrate for the reader what I am saying?

If I realize that my potential readers are likely to be unsympathetic to my viewpoint, I try to help them connect primary beliefs they already hold to primary beliefs in my viewpoint. I try to put myself into their circumstances with their beliefs and outlook. I show them that I understand their perspective.

Writing as Exercise for the Mind

You have a mind. But do you know how to develop it? Are you aware of your basic prejudices and preconceptions? Are you aware of the extent to which your thinking mirrors the thinking of those around you? Are you aware of the extent to which your thinking has been influenced by the thinking of the culture in which you have been raised and conditioned?

In writing about the ideas of others, you can learn to enter the minds of others and appreciate new points of view. In coming to terms with the mind of another, you can come to discover your own mind, both its strengths and its weaknesses. To write the thoughts your mind thinks, you must learn how to do second-order thinking — that is, how to think about your thinking while you are thinking from *outside* your thinking. But how do you get outside your thinking?

To do this, you first must understand that there are eight basic structures to all thinking. Whenever we think, we think for a purpose within a point of view based on assumptions leading to implications and consequences. We use concepts, ideas, and theories to interpret data, facts, and experiences in order to answer questions, solve problems, and resolve issues.

Thinking then:

- has a purpose
- raises questions
- uses information
- utilizes concepts
- makes inferences
- makes assumptions
- generates implications
- embodies a point of view

Elements of Thought

Point of view — frame of reference, perspective, orientation

Purpose — goal, objective

Question at Issue — problem, issue

Information — data, facts, observations, experiences

Interpretation and Inference — conclusions, solutions

Concepts — theories, definitions, axioms, laws, principles, models

Assumptions — presupposition, taking for granted

Implications and Consequences

www.criticalthinking.org

When we take command of these eight basic elements of reasoning, we gain powerful intellectual tools that enable us to think at a higher level. We understand that whenever anyone reasons about anything whatsoever, these parts are inherent in their thinking. Thus, when you write, you inevitably write for a purpose, make inferences, and think within a point of view. At the same time, your readers have a point of view of their own. They have their purposes, their questions, their assumptions, and their beliefs. The better you are at understanding the perspectives of your readers, the better you can understand how to explain your reasoning to them. The better you understand someone else's system of thoughts, the better you can understand your own.

When you can move back and forth effectively between what you are writing and what you want your writing to accomplish, you bring what you are thinking to bear upon what you are writing, and you bring what you are writing to bear upon what you are thinking. You change your writing when you recognize through your thinking that improvement is needed — and how it is needed.

How to Write a Sentence

Within a piece of written work, every sentence should stand in a clear relationship to other sentences. Each sentence, and indeed every word of every sentence, should support the purpose of the written piece.

An important part of writing with discipline is connecting sentences to the broader context within which they are located, seeing how they fit within the whole. For every sentence you write, then, you can ask:

- How does this sentence connect with the other sentences in the paragraph?
- How does this sentence relate to the organizing idea of this text as a whole?

Writing to Learn

Everything we write is a potential learning experience. Writing is a systematic process for learning essential meanings. When we write to become good writers, we teach ourselves as we explain things to others. In fact, teaching through writing is one of the most powerful strategies for learning. When we take core ideas, ideas of substance, and work them into our minds by developing them on paper, they become ideas we can use productively in our lives.

At the same time, to learn well, one must write well. One learns to write well not by writing many things badly, but a few things well.

The few things we should write well are substantive pieces, paragraphs and papers containing important ideas, elaborations that ground our thinking in powerful ideas. It is quite possible to educate oneself entirely through writing, if one has the intellectual skills to work through important texts, enter conflicting viewpoints, internalize important ideas learned, and apply those ideas to one's life. Alternatively, one cannot be an educated person without consistently learning through writing. Why? Because education is a lifelong process that at best begins in school. Without continually integrating new ideas into the ones already established in our thinking, our ideas become stagnant and rigid.

Substantive Writing in Content Areas

To gain knowledge, we must construct it in our minds. Writing what we are trying to internalize helps us achieve that purpose. When we are able to make connections in writing, we begin to take ownership of these connections. To do this, we must learn how to identify core ideas in the books we read, and then explain those ideas in writing, along with the role they play within the subjects we are studying.

All knowledge exists in *systems* of meanings, with interrelated primary, secondary, and peripheral ideas. Imagine a series of circles beginning with a small core circle of primary ideas, surrounded by concentric circles of secondary ideas, moving to an outer circle of peripheral ideas. The primary ideas, at the core, explain the secondary and peripheral ideas. Whenever we read to acquire knowledge, we must write to take ownership, first, of the primary ideas, for they are key to understanding all the other ideas. Furthermore, just as we must write to gain an initial understanding of the primary ideas, we must also write to begin to think within the system as a whole and to make interconnections between ideas. The sooner we begin to think, and therefore write, within a system, the sooner the system becomes meaningful to us.

Thus, when we take command of a core of historical ideas, we begin to think and write historically. When we take command of a core of scientific ideas, we begin to think and write scientifically. Core or primary ideas are the key to every system of knowledge. They are the key to learning any subject. They are the key to retaining what we learn and applying it to life's problems. Without writing about these ideas, they never fully take root in our minds. But by seeking out these ideas and digesting them, we multiply the important subjects we can write about, as well as the multiple important things we can say about them.

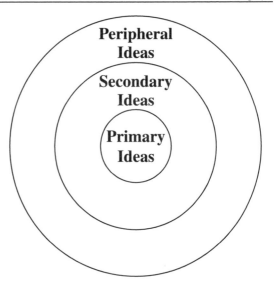

**Essential Idea: Writing
about primary and
secondary ideas
in a discipline is a
key to understanding
the discipline.**

Relating Core Ideas to Other Core Ideas

We should use writing to relate core ideas we learn within one discipline or domain to core ideas in other systems of knowledge, for knowledge exists not only in a system but also in relation to all other systems of knowledge.

Mastering any set of foundational ideas makes it easier to learn other foundational ideas. Learning to think within one system of knowledge helps us learn within other systems. Writing is crucial to that process.

For example, if in studying botany we learn that all plants have cells, we should connect this idea to the fact that all animals have cells (which we learned in studying biology). We then can begin to consider the similarities and differences between the types of animal and plant cells while recognizing a foundational concept that applies to both botany and biology. Or consider the relation between psychology and sociology. Psychology focuses on individual behavior while sociology focuses on group behavior. But people's individual psychology influences how they relate to group norms, and social groups shape how individuals deal with their perceived life problems and opportunities. By putting core ideas within these two disciplines into words, we better understand both fields and therefore can more effectively apply our knowledge to the real world (wherein the psychological and sociological are deeply intertwined).

Writing Within Disciplines

As we have said, to write within subject disciplines, you must recognize that all disciplines are, in fact, *systems* of thought. Indeed, often they are *systems of systems*. Thus, scientific thinking forms a large-scale system of thought (which contrasts with other systems, such as ethical thinking). Science as a large-scale system also contains sub-systems (physics, chemistry, biology, physiology, and so forth). Science, therefore, is a system of systems.

But, unlike science, in which there is agreement on the most basic principles guiding scientific thinking, some systems of systems lack agreement even on their most basic assumptions. For example, the disciplines of philosophy, psychology, and economics are systems of conflicting systems. In contrast to science (wherein all systems work together), philosophical, psychological, and economic systems vie with one another for dominance. Each of these disciplines contains competing *schools* of thought that contradict each other in important ways.

To be an effective writer within disciplines, you must learn to identify (for any given subject) whether it is best understood as a system of supporting systems (such as math and science) or a system of conflicting systems (such as philosophy, psychology, and economics). If you are thinking within a system-harmonious discipline, your task is to master how the systems within it support one another. If you are thinking within a system-conflicting field, your task is to master how and why the systems within it conflict. Of course, in seeing how conflicting systems diverge, you also discover how they overlap. Conflict between systems of thought is rarely, if ever, total and absolute.

To test your knowledge of any given system of thought, you should be able to state, elaborate, exemplify, and illustrate the most fundamental concept within that system. For example, if you are studying science, you should be able to, at minimum, write your understanding of what science is in a way that would satisfy scientists. If you are studying history, or indeed any other field of study, you should be able to do the same. You should be able, as well, to explain in writing how fundamental concepts between disciplines overlap or conflict.

The Work of Writing

Writing, then, is a form of intellectual work. And intellectual work requires a willingness to persevere through difficulties. But perhaps even more important, good writing requires understanding what intellectual work is and how it relates to writing. This is where most students fall short. Here is an illustration: Creating a paragraph well is like building a house. You need a foundation, and everything else must be built upon that foundation. The house must have at least one entrance, and it must be apparent to people where that entrance is. The first floor must fit the foundation, and the second floor must match up with the first, with some stairway that enables us to get from the first floor to the second.

Building a house involves the work of both design and construction. Each is essential. No one would expect students to automatically know how to design and construct houses. But sometimes we approach writing as if knowledge of how to design and write a paragraph or a paper were apparent to all students.

Questioning as We Write

Skilled writers approach writing as an active dialogue involving questioning. They question as they write. They question to understand. They question to evaluate what they are writing. They question to bring important ideas into their thinking. Here are some of the questions good writers ask while writing:

- Why am I writing this? What is my purpose? What do I want the reader to come away with?

- Is there some part of what I have written that I don't really understand? Perhaps I am repeating what I have heard people say without ever having thought through what exactly it means.

- If something I have written is vague, how can I make it clearer or more precise?

- Do I understand the meaning of the key words I have used, or do I need to look them up in the dictionary?

- Am I using any words in special or unusual ways? Have I explained special meanings to the reader?

- Am I sure that what I have said is accurate? Do I need to qualify anything?

Continued ➜

- Am I clear about my main point and why I think it is important?
- Do I know what question my paragraph answers?
- Do I need to spend more time investigating my topic or issue? Do I need more information?

If a person tries to write without understanding what writing involves, the writing will likely be poor. For example, many students see writing as a fundamentally passive activity. Their theory of writing seems to be something like this: "You write whatever comes to your mind, sentence by sentence, until you have written the assigned length."

By contrast, the work of substantive writing is the work of first choosing (constructing) a subject worth writing about and then thinking through (constructing) something worth saying about that subject. It is a highly selective activity. Five intellectual acts required for developing substance in your writing are:

- Choose a subject or idea of importance.
- Decide on something important to say about it.
- Explain or elaborate your basic meaning.
- Construct examples that will help readers connect what you are saying to events and experiences in their lives.
- Construct one or more analogies and/or metaphors that will help readers connect what you are writing about with something similar in their lives.

Non-Substantive Writing

It is possible to learn to write with an emphasis on style, variety of sentence structure, and rhetorical principles without learning to write in a substantive manner. Rhetorically powerful writing may be, and in our culture often is, intellectually bankrupt. Many intellectually impoverished thinkers write well in the purely rhetorical sense. Propaganda, for one, is often expressed in a rhetorically effective way. Political speeches empty of significant content are often rhetorically well-designed. Sophistry and self-delusion often thrive in rhetorically proficient prose.

A *New York Times* special supplement on education (Aug. 4, 2002) included a description of a new section in the SAT focused on a "20-minute writing exercise." The prompt those taking the test were asked to write on was as follows: "There is always a however." One might as justifiably ask a person to write on the theme, "There is always an always!" Or "There is never a never!" Such writing prompts are the equivalent of an intellectual Rorschach inkblot. They do not define a clear intellectual task. There is no issue to be reasoned through. Thus, the writer is encouraged to pontificate using rhetorical and stylistic devises rather than reason using intellectual good sense, to talk about nothing as if it is something.

Substantive writing requires that the writer begin with a significant, intellectually well-defined task. This writing can be assessed for clarity, accuracy, relevance, depth, breadth, logic, significance, and fairness (rather than rhetorical style and flourish). Substantive writing enables the author to take ownership of ideas worth understanding. There are numerous possibilities for designing such a writing task. We shall exemplify some basic options next.

The Practice
Exercises in Substantive Writing

You now know something about the theory of substantive writing. In the discussion that follows, you will be given strategies for practicing substantive writing. Each form of practice will help you write more substantively: to identify subjects worth talking about, to say something worth saying about them, and to say what you have to say clearly and precisely. Substantive writing requires that the writer know where she is beginning, where she is going, and how she is getting there.

The foundations of substantive writing are based on foundational critical thinking principles and concepts — for example, on the elements and standards of thought. The elements of thought enable us to break down thought into its constituent parts (purpose, question, information, inference, concept, assumption, implication, point of view). Standards of thought enable us to evaluate thought (for clarity, accuracy, precision, relevance, depth, breadth, logic, significance, fairness). Knowing how to analyze and evaluate thinking is essential to substantive writing. These critical thinking processes are utilized in the final two sets of exercises in this section.

To introduce examples of substantive thought, we have identified and include in this section some classic texts and quotations. We use them as a springboard to substantive writing. If one can take a substantive text and capture its essential meaning in writing (using one's own words and thoughts), one has begun the process of writing substantively.

Most of the exercises in this section require the use of the most prominent critical thinking strategy for clarification — to state, elaborate, exemplify, and illustrate a thought. The essential first steps in learning to write substantively are (1) to find a subject worth writing about, (2) to discover something significant to say about it, and (3) to express oneself clearly and precisely. To think well, we must at least think clearly. Confused and muddled thinking are never the basis for either knowledge or understanding.

Paraphrasing — putting into your own words — what a sentence or text is saying is at the heart of what we are advocating. When one can say what great minds have thought, one can think what great minds have said. Analysis and evaluation are a logical follow-up to paraphrasing.

We provide a variety of templates for practice. Some of these exercises are easier than others. If you decide that any given exercise is too challenging, pass it by and work on others, then come back to the difficult ones later. Our goal is to help you proceed from the simple to the complex, but what is simple for one person is sometimes complex to another.

Finally, we do not have the space to exemplify all possible patterns of substantive writing. But the patterns we do provide are basic and, when routinely practiced, lead to a progressively deeper understanding of substantive thinking, learning, and writing.

Paraphrasing

According to the *Oxford English Dictionary*, to "paraphrase" is *to express the meaning of a word, phrase, passage, or work in other words, usually with the object of fuller and clearer exposition*. To the extent that we cannot state in our own words the meaning of a word, sentence, or passage, we lack an understanding of that word, sentence, or passage. We bring ideas into our thinking by "thinking them into our thinking." One of the best ways to do this is to practice paraphrasing — writing in our own words our understanding of an idea, sentence, or passage.

This is easier said than done. To paraphrase a substantive sentence or passage effectively, the writer must come to think, and appreciate, the substantive thought behind the sentence or passage. Without this appreciation, without deeply understanding the thought expressed in the original, one cannot render that thought adequately in different words.

The human mind can understand a *deep* thought at varying levels of depth. Many will say, for example, that they understand the thought, "A little learning is a dangerous thing," when subsequent discussion proves that they do not appreciate it — for example, when they fail to see how it applies to their life. The fact is that few have had practice in paraphrasing substantive sentences and passages. Few have thought about the significance of the art of paraphrasing. Few understand its essential connection to substantive learning.

To appreciate fine painting or music or novels or poems or any other domain of intellectual creativity, we must experience them in multiple forms. An insightful paraphrase of an important text provides an initial sense of one way to think the thought in that text, for a paraphrase re-creates an original thought in new words. To select the words that do the job, one must struggle with the thought and with possible words as candidates to express it.

To re-phrase a powerful thought adequately, it is usually necessary to express it in a more extended form. That is why paraphrasing a thought is sometimes called *unpacking* it. The original is compact. The paraphrase takes it apart and lays out the elements — and therefore expresses it in *more*, rather than *fewer*, words.

There is, it should be clear, no exact form of paraphrase. Most substantial thoughts can be captured by a variety of formulations — each giving us a different angle of vision. Practice in paraphrasing is, therefore, practice in taking ownership of thinking that stretches the mind, thinking that brings us to deeper and deeper levels of understanding. In a world of glorified superficiality, disciplined practice in paraphrasing significant thought is rare.

Now consider the four questions that can be used to assess writing for clarity:

1. Could you *state* your basic point in one simple sentence?
2. Could you *elaborate* your basic point more fully (in other words)?
3. Could you give me an *example* of your point from your experience?
4. Could you give me an *analogy* or metaphor to help me see what you mean?

Each of these clarification strategies requires a substantive writing skill. You will be developing these abilities and others in the writing exercises in this section.

Clarification Strategies

- **The ability to state a thesis clearly in a sentence.** If we cannot accurately state our key idea in a sentence using our own words, we don't really know what we want to say.

- **The ability to explain a thesis sentence in greater detail.** If we cannot elaborate our key idea, then we have not yet connected its meaning to other concepts that we understand.

- **The ability to give examples of what we are saying.** If we cannot connect what we have elaborated with concrete situations in the real world, our knowledge of the meanings is still abstract, and, to some extent, vague.

- **The ability to illustrate what we are saying with a metaphor, analogy, picture, diagram, or drawing.** If we cannot generate metaphors, analogies, pictures, or diagrams of the meanings we are constructing, we have not yet connected what we understand with other domains of knowledge and experience.

Sample Paraphrases

Consider the following sample paraphrases before we move on to more detailed paraphrasing:

He who passively accepts evil is as much involved in it as he who helps to perpetuate it. — *Martin Luther King, Jr.*

People who see unethical things being done to others but who fail to intervene (when they are able to intervene) are as unethical as those who are causing harm in the first place.

Every effort to confine Americanism to a single pattern, to constrain it to a single formula, is disloyalty to everything that is valid in Americanism. — *Henry Steele Commager*

There is no one "right way" to be an American. When everyone in America is expected to think within one belief system, when people are ostracized or persecuted for thinking autonomously, when people are labeled "UnAmerican" for independent thinking, the only legitimate definition of "true American" is annulled.

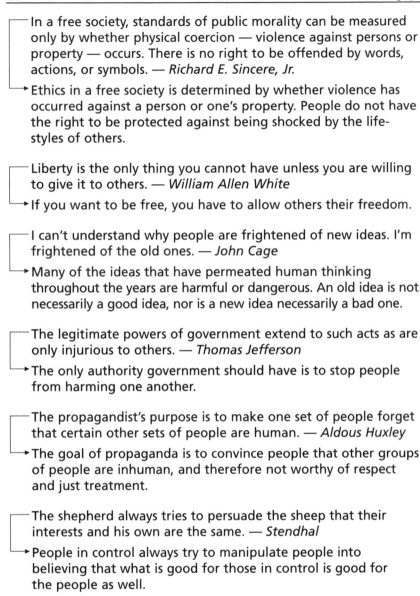

In a free society, standards of public morality can be measured only by whether physical coercion — violence against persons or property — occurs. There is no right to be offended by words, actions, or symbols. — *Richard E. Sincere, Jr.*

Ethics in a free society is determined by whether violence has occurred against a person or one's property. People do not have the right to be protected against being shocked by the life-styles of others.

Liberty is the only thing you cannot have unless you are willing to give it to others. — *William Allen White*

If you want to be free, you have to allow others their freedom.

I can't understand why people are frightened of new ideas. I'm frightened of the old ones. — *John Cage*

Many of the ideas that have permeated human thinking throughout the years are harmful or dangerous. An old idea is not necessarily a good idea, nor is a new idea necessarily a bad one.

The legitimate powers of government extend to such acts as are only injurious to others. — *Thomas Jefferson*

The only authority government should have is to stop people from harming one another.

The propagandist's purpose is to make one set of people forget that certain other sets of people are human. — *Aldous Huxley*

The goal of propaganda is to convince people that other groups of people are inhuman, and therefore not worthy of respect and just treatment.

The shepherd always tries to persuade the sheep that their interests and his own are the same. — *Stendhal*

People in control always try to manipulate people into believing that what is good for those in control is good for the people as well.

Paraphrasing Short Quotes

One way to paraphrase quotes is to begin by writing out your *initial thoughts*. Then paraphrase the quote in the light of your commentary. In your commentary, explain the significance of what is being talked about and what is being said. If there is an important concept at the heart of the quote — a concept such as democracy or power as in the two example quotes below — think through that concept before you paraphrase.

First Exercise

In this section we present you with short quotes based on significant insights. We want you to paraphrase each one. But first write out your initial thoughts. When paraphrasing try to use more, rather than less elaboration to unpack the ideas in the quote. We provide two examples, but without initial thoughts.

Example One

Quote: "Democracy is rule by the people."

Possible Paraphrase: Democracy exists only to the extent that there is a broad basis of equality of political power among the people at large. This means that all people within the state should have relatively equal power and equal input in determining what the laws will be. By implication, a state fails to be democratic to the extent that a few people — whether they be wealthy or otherwise influential — have more power than others.

Example Two

Quote: "Power corrupts, and absolute power corrupts absolutely."

Possible Paraphrase: The more control people gain over the lives of others, the greater is their propensity to exploit those people, and their consequent loss of personal integrity and honesty.

Now it is your turn to practice, using the quotes that follow:

Quote: "If a man empties his purse into his head, no man can take it away from him. An investment in knowledge always pays the best interest." — *Benjamin Franklin*

Possible Paraphrase:

Quote: "Universal suffrage, without universal education, would be a curse." — *H. L. Wayland*
Possible Paraphrase:

Quote: "The school should always have as its aim that the young leave it as a harmonious personality, not as a specialist... The development of general ability for independent thinking and judgment should always be placed foremost, not the acquisition of special knowledge." — *Albert Einstein*

Possible Paraphrase:

Quote: "Do not ask if a man has been through college; ask if a college has been through him — if he is a walking university."
— *E. H. Chapin*
Possible Paraphrase:

In this activity, you have interpreted important quotes by paraphrasing them. In the next activity you will practice another way of approaching deep understanding of important texts.

Second Exercise

Use the following template to guide you in explicating the following quotes:

1. The essence of this quote is...

2. In other words...

3. For example...

4. To give you a metaphor (or analogy) so you can better understand what I am saying...

Example

"All truly wise thoughts have been thought already thousands of times; but to make them truly ours, we must think them over again honestly, till they take root in our personal experience."
— *Goethe*

1. *The essence of this quote is* that the most important ideas are not new, but what is new is using them in our thinking. We have to think them through for ourselves, again and again, until we can use them in our lives.

2. *In other words*, we don't have to be brilliant to use significant ideas in our life. All of the most important ideas have already been figured out and thought through numerous times throughout history. But if we want to take possession of these ideas, we have to be committed to working them into our thinking, connecting them to personal experience, and then using them to guide our behavior. If we want to live better lives, we don't have to come up with novel or original ideas. Rather, we need to learn how to live the ones already available to us.

3. *For example* consider what Socrates proposed (around 600 B.C.): *The unexamined life is not worth living*. Throughout history, many people have said that if you want to improve your life, you have to look at the way you live; you have to think about your behavior and what causes you to behave irrationally. Yet, few people take this idea seriously. Few have thought about what it would mean to examine their life. Few have any tools for doing this. Few have related this idea to their personal experience. Few have really faced themselves straight on.

4. *To give you a metaphor (or analogy) so you can better understand what I am saying*, consider this: Every city has libraries containing thousands of books that express important ideas and experiences. Yet, most of these books are ignored, not read. Few think of the library as a place to gain ideas that can change their lives for the better. Few realize that rather than to seek out a flashy (and probably superficial) *new* idea from the mass media, they should master some of the many *old*, time-tested, deep, and important ideas (from a library or good bookstore).

Now it's your turn.

Use the structure outlined on page 18 to write substantively about the following quotes:

"No man is free who is not master of himself." — *Epictetus*

"All our freedoms are a single bundle; all must be secure if any is to be preserved." — *Dwight D. Eisenhower*

"None are more hopelessly enslaved than those who falsely believe they are free." — *Goethe*

"Security is never an absolute... The government of a free people must take certain chances for the sake of maintaining freedom which the government of a police state avoids." — *Bartholini*

"The first step to knowledge is to know that we are ignorant." — *Cecil*

"The more you practice what you know, the more shall you know what to practice." — *W. Jenkin*

"What is not fully understood is not possessed." — *Goethe*

"If you would thoroughly know anything, teach it to others." — *Tyron Edwards*

"The mind is but a barren soil...unless it be continually fertilized and enriched with foreign matter." — *Sir J. Reynolds*

"What stubbing, plowing, digging, and harrowing is to land, that thinking, reflecting, examining is to the mind." — *Berkeley*

"Don't despair of a student if he has one clear idea." — *Nathaniel Emmons*

"Narrow minds think nothing right that is beyond their own capacity." — *Rochefoucauld*

"There is no more independence in politics than there is in jail." — *Will Rogers*

"If you wish the sympathy of broad masses then you must tell them the crudest and most stupid things." — *Adolf Hitler*

"Two kinds of men generally best succeed in political life: men of no principle, but of great talent: and men of no talent; but of one principle — that of obedience to their superiors." — *Wendell Phillips*

"Justice without power is inefficient; power without justice is tyranny." — *Pascal*

"Power is ever stealing from the many to the few." — *Wendell Phillips*

"Power, like the diamond, dazzles the beholder, and also the wearer; it dignifies meanness; it magnifies littleness; to what is contemptible, it gives authority; to what is low, exaltation." — *Charles Caleb Colton*

"Even legal punishments lose all appearance of justice, when too strictly inflicted on men compelled by the last extremity of distress to incur them." — *Junius*

"Thinking is the hardest work there is, which is the probable reason why so few engage in it." — *Henry Ford*

"Thought engenders thought. Place one idea upon paper, another will follow it, and still another, until you have written a page… Learn to think, and you will learn to write; the more you think, the better you will express your ideas." — *G.A. Sala*

"Our thoughts are ours, their ends none of our own." — *William Shakespeare*

"All truly wise thoughts have been thought already thousands of times; but to make them truly ours, we must think them over again honestly, till they take root in our personal experience." — *Goethe*

"The key to every man is his thought." — *Ralph Waldo Emerson*

Extended Paraphrases

In the next section we focus on three substantive passages that have influenced the thinking of many reflective persons. Your job is to re-capture the thinking within the passage by expressing it in your own words. After you paraphrase the passages sentence by sentence, you can read our sample interpretations. We then provide examples of how one might explicate the thesis of the passage using the clarification format previously introduced. Construct your own explication before reading our example. The appendices include additional models you can use for further practice.

Paraphrasing and Clarifying Substantive Texts

Directions: For each of the three texts that follow, test your grasp of the passages by putting them into your own words. Compare your writing with the sample interpretation that follows the *First Exercise: Paraphrasing* Section.

Man's Search for Meaning

Background Information: The following excerpt is taken from Viktor E. Frankl's book, *Man's Search for Meaning* (1959). Dr. Frankl, a psychiatrist and neurologist who was imprisoned at Auschwitz and other Nazi prisons, developed a theory of "logotherapy" which "focuses its attention upon mankind's groping for a higher meaning in life."

What man actually needs is not a tensionless state but rather the striving and struggling for some goal worthy of him. What he needs is not the discharge of tension at any cost, but the call of a potential meaning waiting to be fulfilled by him… [People] lack the awareness of a meaning worth living for. They are haunted by the experience of their inner emptiness, a void within themselves; they are caught in that situation which I have called the 'existential vacuum.'…This existential vacuum manifests itself mainly in a state of boredom… Not a few cases of suicide can be traced back to this existential vacuum… Sometimes the frustrated will to meaning is vicariously compensated for by a will to power, including the most primitive form of the will to power, the will to money. In other cases, the place of frustrated will to meaning is taken by the will to pleasure... Ultimately, man should not ask what the meaning of life is, but rather must recognize that it is *he* who is asked. In a word, each meaning is questioned by life; and he can only answer to life by *answering* for his own life; to life he can only respond by being responsible... (pp. 166-172).

First Exercise: Paraphrasing

What man actually needs is not a tensionless state but rather the striving and struggling for some goal worthy of him. What he needs is not the discharge of tension at any cost, but the call of a potential meaning waiting to be fulfilled by him...

PARAPHRASE:

[People] lack the awareness of a meaning worth living for. They are haunted by the experience of their inner emptiness, a void within themselves; they are caught in that situation which I have called the 'existential vacuum.'...

PARAPHRASE:

This existential vacuum manifests itself mainly in a state of boredom... Not a few cases of suicide can be traced back to this existential vacuum...

PARAPHRASE:

Sometimes the frustrated will to meaning is vicariously compensated for by a will to power, including the most primitive form of the will to power, the will to money. In other cases, the place of frustrated will to meaning is taken by the will to pleasure…

PARAPHRASE:

Ultimately, man should not ask what the meaning of life is, but rather must recognize that it is *he* who is asked.

PARAPHRASE:

In a word, each meaning is questioned by life; and he can only answer to life by *answering* for his own life; to life he can only respond by being responsible…

PARAPHRASE:

Compare Your Writing: Sample Interpretation

What man actually needs is not a tensionless state but rather the striving and struggling for some goal worthy of him. What he needs is not the discharge of tension at any cost, but the call of a potential meaning waiting to be fulfilled by him…

Paraphrase: People should not strive to be without stress and challenge. Rather they should actively seek important purposes. People shouldn't spend their time and energy simply trying to relieve pressure in their lives. Instead they should use their energy seeking out pursuits that are significant and important to them.

[People] lack the awareness of a meaning worth living for. They are haunted by the experience of their inner emptiness, a void within themselves; they are caught in that situation which I have called the 'existential vacuum.'…

Paraphrase: People often do not see that there is anything significant in life. Their minds are not actively pursing anything interesting, anything that gives them deep meaning in their lives. Life seems barren and unfulfilling.

This existential vacuum manifests itself mainly in a state of boredom… Not a few cases of suicide can be traced back to this existential vacuum…

Paraphrase: This lack of significant meaning in one's life often leads to tedium, dullness, apathy, indifference. Even suicide is sometimes caused by a state of "empty existence."

Sometimes the frustrated will to meaning is vicariously compensated for by a will to power, including the most primitive form of the will to power, the will to money. In other cases, the place of frustrated will to meaning is taken by the will to pleasure…

Paraphrase: Sometimes when people fail to pursue important meanings and goals, their energy is used instead in the pursuit of control and domination. Some even resort to the most crude type of power, that of pursuing wealth simply for the sake of wealth. In still other persons, the failure to pursue important objectives is covered over by a vain pursuit of pleasure.

Ultimately, man should not ask what the meaning of life is, but rather must recognize that it is *he* who is asked. In a word, each meaning is questioned by life; and he can only answer to life by *answering* for his own life; to life he can only respond by being responsible…

Paraphrase: In the final analysis people should not try to figure out *the* meaning of life. Instead they should answer the questions: "What meaning can I give to my own life? What important meaning can I create for myself? What goals can I pursue that make my life important?" In short, people have to answer to the world for their actions. Each of us must justify how and why we are living our lives the way we do. And each of us is responsible to pursue important goals, to live in a conscientious way. Each of us is accountable for the life-forming decisions we make. Each of us is responsible for our own well-being.

Second Exercise:
Thesis of *Man's Search for Meaning*

Directions: Complete the following four tasks: (1) State the thesis of the passage in your own words. (2) Elaborate the thesis. (3) Give one or more examples of the thesis. (4) Illustrate the thesis with a metaphor or analogy.

Statement of Thesis

The only way to live a truly meaningful life is to seek important purposes and live in accordance with those purposes.

Elaboration of Thesis

Most people have no sense of how to find important meanings for their lives. Instead, they are bored with life. They ask questions like: "What is *the* meaning of life?" In its place they should ask, "What important meanings can I create for myself?" In short, people tend to look outside themselves for pre-designed meaning instead of selecting from a range of challenging and important goals for themselves.

Exemplification of Thesis

Rather than seeking objectives that would be truly fulfilling, people often pursue power, money, fun, and excitement. When people pursue power, for example, they funnel their energy into that which enables them to control other people, to see themselves as superior to others. This substitutes for a truly fulfilling meaning in life. But when people develop meaningful, rational purposes, they become much more satisfied with life. Many teenagers lack important purposes. They are looking for instant gratification. They are seeking fun and excitement in superficial relationships and events. Because this lifestyle doesn't lead to any important meaning in their lives, they often turn to drugs and alcohol for cheap thrills. Alternatively, when teenagers pursue activities and goals that are important to them (e.g., sports, photography, writing, political causes, drama) they find true meaning in their lives. They aren't bored with life. They don't need to be accepted by their peer group. They use their energy to create something they see as important to them personally.

Illustration of Thesis

Seeking important meanings in life is like seeking a pearl in an oyster. The oyster is like the stuff of life that can keep us from identifying important goals, the stuff that gets in the way of the prize that is worth the seeking. It is the dull grayish brown substance that easily entraps us. We have to work through the oyster to get to the pearl. We have to work through difficulties to find what is really important to us. But the reward is brilliant and shiny, and true (to who and what we are).

History of the Great American Fortunes

Background Understandings: In 1909, Gustavus Myers wrote a three-volume history of the great American fortunes. At the time Myers was attempting to understand and then explain how the wealthiest people in the country obtained their wealth. In his book, he focuses neither on extraordinary ability or hard work on the part of these people, nor does he directly connect this vast wealth to greed or lack of ethics. Rather he contends that "the great fortunes are the natural, logical outcome of a system."…[a system producing] "the utter despoilment of the many for the benefit of a few." The result is a "natural" economic and human result. As he put it, "…our plutocrats rank as nothing more or less than so many unavoidable creations of a set of processes which must imperatively produce a certain set of results." The following excerpt is from the first chapter of his book, *History of the Great American Fortunes:*

The noted private fortunes of settlement and colonial times were derived from the ownership of land and the gains of trading. …Through-out the colonies were scattered lords of the soil who had vast territorial domains over which they exercised an arbitrary and, in some portions of the colonies, a feudal sway… Nearly all the colonies were settled by chartered companies, organized for purely commercial purposes and the success of which largely depended upon the emigration which they were able to promote.

These corporations were vested with enormous powers and privileges which, in effect, constituted them as sovereign rulers…

As the demands of commerce had to be sustained at any price, a system was at once put into operation of gathering in as many of the poorer English class as could be impressed upon some pretext, and shipping them over to be held as bonded laborers. Penniless and lowly Englishmen, arrested and convicted for any one of the multitude of offenses then provided for severely in law,

> were transported as criminals or sold into the colonies as slaves for a term of years. The English courts were busy grinding out human material for the Virginia Plantation… No voice was raised in protest (pp. 11–12).

First Exercise: Paraphrasing

The noted private fortunes of settlement and colonial times were derived from the ownership of land and the gains of trading.

PARAPHRASE:

…Through-out the colonies were scattered lords of the soil who had vast territorial domains over which they exercised an arbitrary and, in some portions of the colonies, a feudal sway…

PARAPHRASE:

Nearly all the colonies were settled by chartered companies, organized for purely commercial purposes and the success of which largely depended upon the emigration which they were able to promote.

PARAPHRASE:

These corporations were vested with enormous powers and privileges which, in effect, constituted them as sovereign rulers…

PARAPHRASE:

As the demands of commerce had to be sustained at any price, a system was at once put into operation of gathering in as many of the poorer English class as could be impressed upon some pretext, and shipping them over to be held as bonded laborers.

PARAPHRASE:

Penniless and lowly Englishmen, arrested and convicted for any one of the multitude of offenses then provided for severely in law, were transported as criminals or sold into the colonies as slaves for a term of years. The English courts were busy grinding out human material for the Virginia Plantation…

PARAPHRASE:

No voice was raised in protest.

PARAPHRASE:

Compare Your Writing: Sample Interpretation

The noted private fortunes of settlement and colonial times were derived from the ownership of land and the gains of trading.

PARAPHRASE: During the time of the early American colonies, the wealthy people got their wealth from owning land and engaging in trade.

…Through-out the colonies were scattered lords of the soil who had vast territorial domains over which they exercised an arbitrary and, in some portions of the colonies, a feudal sway…

PARAPHRASE: Everywhere in the colonies there were people with huge estates so large and powerful, so great that these land owners were virtual "lords" who could command almost anything they wanted of the people who lived in their province, as medieval lords could.

Nearly all the colonies were settled by chartered companies, organized for purely commercial purposes and the success of which largely depended upon the emigration which they were able to promote.

PARAPHRASE: Almost all the people who took over these territories from the Native Americans did so through licensed companies. These companies were concerned with nothing but profit. Their success depended on getting people to come from other lands.

These corporations were vested with enormous powers and privileges which, in effect, constituted them as sovereign rulers...
PARAPHRASE: The companies so formed had stupendous power and rights that rendered them autonomous and virtually self-governing.

As the demands of commerce had to be sustained at any price, a system was at once put into operation of gathering in as many of the poorer English class as could be impressed upon some pretext, and shipping them over to be held as bonded laborers.
PARAPHRASE: Because profit was their only ultimate motive and the system they set up required cheap labor, England began the practice of devising excuses that justified forcing poor people to come to the colonies as near slaves.

Penniless and lowly Englishmen, arrested and convicted for any one of the multitude of offenses then provided for severely in law, were transported as criminals or sold into the colonies as slaves for a term of years. The English courts were busy grinding out human material for the Virginia Plantation...
PARAPHRASE: The English court-system became the economic vehicle that enabled the wealthy colonial companies and their masters to gather and use masses of poor people for their vested interests. The system was set up so that for any number of reasons the poor could be found guilty of any of a number of offenses and punished severely. This punishment often consisted of sending them off to the colonies as slaves for a specified number of years.

No voice was raised in protest.
PARAPHRASE: Virtually no one objected to this cruel and unethical system.

Second Exercise: Thesis of the
History of the Great American Fortunes

Statement of Thesis

A minority of persons in the early American colonies acquired vast fortunes, land, and power through the exploitation of poor people in England.

Elaboration of Thesis

The dominant form of government in the early American colonies was not democracy but something more like feudal oligarchy. Relatively few wealthy colonists were at the pinnacle of a system of powerful licensed companies that had acquired from the English King complete power and authority to rule a region and the people in it. Profit was the overriding end. The systematic denial of human rights for those manipulated and used by the powerful was standard practice and went virtually unquestioned.

Exemplification of Thesis

For example, people were accused and convicted of petty crimes in England for the tacit purpose of providing virtual slaves for the colonies. (These convicts were sentenced into forced labor for the companies authorized by the King.)

Illustration of Thesis

To better understand this phenomenon, we might consider the legal institution of slavery in America from the 1600s until the 1800s. Innocent Africans were rounded up and sold into slavery for one explicit purpose — the pursuit of wealth by land-owners. By using free forced labor, the rich got richer and the slaves were denied their most fundamental human rights. The same denial of rights was inherent in the system that convicted poor people in England to a life of virtual slavery to American land-owners.

On Liberty

Background Information: The following excerpt is taken from
H. L. Mencken's book series entitled *Prejudices* (1919–1927).
Mencken's work is highly acclaimed by scholars for its literary, social
and political critique. Mencken is arguably the most distinguished
journalist in United States history.

I believe in liberty. And when I say liberty, I mean the
thing in its widest imaginable sense — liberty up to the
extreme limits of the feasible and tolerable. I am against
forbidding anybody to do anything, or say anything, or
think anything so long as it is at all possible to imagine a
habitable world in which he would be free to do, say, and
think it. The burden of proof, as I see it, is always upon
the policeman, which is to say, upon the lawmaker, the
theologian, the right-thinker. He must prove his case
doubly, triply, quadruply, and then he must start all over
and prove it again. The eye through which I view him is
watery and jaundiced. I do not pretend to be "just" to him
— any more than a Christian pretends to be just to the
devil. He is the enemy of everything I admire and respect
in this world — of everything that makes it various and
amusing and charming. He impedes every honest search
for the truth. He stands against every sort of good-will
and common decency. His ideal is that of an animal
trainer, an archbishop, a major general in the army. I am
against him until the last galoot's ashore (pp. 193–194).

First Exercise: Paraphrasing

I believe in liberty. And when I say liberty, I mean the thing in its
widest imaginable sense — liberty up to the extreme limits of the
feasible and tolerable.

PARAPHRASE:

I am against forbidding anybody to do anything, or say anything, or think anything so long as it is at all possible to imagine a habitable world in which he would be free to do, say, and think it.

PARAPHRASE:

The burden of proof, as I see it, is always upon the policeman, which is to say, upon the lawmaker, the theologian, the right-thinker. He must prove his case doubly, triply, quadruply, and then he must start all over and prove it again.

PARAPHRASE:

The eye through which I view him is watery and jaundiced. I do not pretend to be "just" to him — any more than a Christian pretends to be just to the devil.

PARAPHRASE:

He is the enemy of everything I admire and respect in this world — of everything that makes it various and amusing and charming. He impedes every honest search for the truth.

PARAPHRASE:

He stands against every sort of good-will and common decency. His ideal is that of an animal trainer, an archbishop, a major general in the army.

PARAPHRASE:

I am against him until the last galoot's ashore.

PARAPHRASE:

Compare Your Writing: Sample Interpretation

I believe in liberty. And when I say liberty, I mean the thing in its widest imaginable sense — liberty up to the extreme limits of the feasible and tolerable.

Paraphrase: I believe in freedom. By this I mean that people should be absolutely as free as possible to do what they want, to live life as they choose. The only freedoms people shouldn't have are those that cannot be supported by a civil society (because they deny someone else a fundamental right).

I am against forbidding anybody to do anything, or say anything, or think anything so long as it is at all possible to imagine a habitable world in which he would be free to do, say, and think it.

Paraphrase: I believe that people should be given the right to say what they choose, to think what they choose, to do what they choose as long as people can at all get along while they have these rights.

The burden of proof, as I see it, is always upon the policeman, which is to say, upon the lawmaker, the theologian, the right-thinker. He must prove his case doubly, triply, quadruply, and then he must start all over and prove it again.

Paraphrase: Anyone arguing against the fundamental rights to say, think, and do as one chooses, must prove beyond any doubt that these rights must be denied someone for unquestionable reasons. The burden of proof falls, not on those accused of some wrong-doing, but on accusers, on police officers, politicians who create laws, religious leaders, and righteous people (i.e., people who see themselves as possessing *the truth*). These accusers must prove unequivocally that one deserves to be denied one's fundamental rights, and they must prove it not only once, but twice, three times, four times, and then yet another time. In other words, they must prove it beyond any doubt whatsoever.

The eye through which I view him is watery and jaundiced. I do not pretend to be "just" to him — any more than a Christian pretends to be just to the devil.

Paraphrase: I am cynical, pessimistic, and skeptical about people who see themselves as possessing *the truth* and who inflict their righteous views on others. Because they deny people their rights to think and do as they choose, I see them as unjust. Therefore I openly refuse to treat their views equal to views that support fundamental human rights.

He is the enemy of everything I admire and respect in this world — of everything that makes it various and amusing and charming.
Paraphrase: Righteous thinking that would deny someone their basic rights goes against everything that is good in the world, everything I hold in high esteem, everything that is honorable. Without differing views and differing ways of living, life would be boring, uninteresting, dull.

He impedes every honest search for the truth. He stands against every sort of good-will and common decency. His ideal is that of an animal trainer, an archbishop, a major general in the army.
Paraphrase: Because they see themselves as possessing *the truth*, righteous thinkers get in the way of figuring out what is actually going on in a situation or what makes sense to believe. They don't seek the truth, but rather distort the truth according to their belief systems. They routinely act in bad-faith. They lack integrity and are, in sum, unethical. They want to rule and dominate people, and they expect people to accept their domination submissively.

I am against him until the last galoot's ashore.
Paraphrase: I am absolutely against these righteous, holier-than-thou thinkers until the last foolish or uncouth person comes to this country (which will be never, because some foolish and uncouth people will always be arriving).

Second Exercise: Thesis of *On Liberty*

Statement of Thesis
As long as they are not actually harming others, people should be allowed to say what they want, think what they want, and do what they want. This is what it means to live in a free, civilized society.

Elaboration of Thesis
There are many righteous people who believe that the way they think and act are the only *correct* ways to think and act. These people are narrow-minded in view, and they expect everyone else to see things as they do. They do not allow for autonomous

thought. Moreover, these people are often in positions of authority. In order to maintain individual liberties as espoused in a free society, people with authority over others (such as police, judges, social workers, politicians who create laws), when attempting to take away someone's rights, must always prove beyond any doubt that this action is the only reasonable way to deal with the situation. But people in these positions of authority are often self-righteous, unable to look at life from multiple perspectives. They therefore cannot be trusted either to see what is right in a situation or to do what is right.

Exemplification of Thesis

For example, some "Child Protective Services" workers profess to be concerned with the well-being of children, while at the same time ignoring information that would help them best serve the child. For instance, in some cases, children have been taken away from their parents simply because the CPS worker thought the parent's didn't keep the house as clean as they thought it should be kept. At the same time, children taken into state custody often fare much worse than they would have done if they had stayed with their parents (due to the dismal conditions of many foster care programs). People in positions of authority often use their prejudices to determine what is right in the situation. Without knowing it, they often impose their personal beliefs and value judgments on others, as if their own views were part of the law.

Illustration of Thesis

To illustrate the point that Mencken makes in this passage, imagine a bird soaring through the air, free to go wherever he chooses whenever he chooses. Then imagine that bird harnessed, entrapped, caged in by those more powerful. People, like birds, are meant to fly free, to live according to their own desires, to develop unique thoughts, to pursue personal ideals. Our distinctive and individual ways of taking flight, our varying destinations, our alternative viewpoints are what makes living interesting. When this natural freedom is denied us, we, like the trapped bird, find ourselves in a cage, everyone unable to fly, all expected to act in the same narrow-minded, judgmental way.

Exploring Conflicting Ideas

In the next section we present you with a group of conflicting ideas, ideas significant in human life. By developing commentary on the ideas and working out the relationships between them, you will find yourself engaged in substantive writing.

Exercise

In the following exercises the focus is on identifying and writing in a disciplined way about ideas that conflict with one another. Use the following structure:

1. Find two important potentially conflicting ideas. These ideas may be embedded in a text or not. The text may be literary, political, economic, ethical, scientific, personal, sociological, historical, and so forth: freedom vs. law; democracy vs. wealth; power vs. justice; passion vs. objectivity; love vs. control; loyalty vs. prejudice; fact vs. ideology; freedom vs. tradition; new vs. old; nationalism vs. internationalism; politician vs. statesman; ideal vs. real.

2. Express an important problem that exists because of one conflict between the ideas you have selected.

3. Decide on an important point to make about that idea. This is your thesis.

4. Elaborate your thesis.

5. Exemplify your thesis.

6. Illustrate your thesis.

7. Formulate at least one reasonable objection to your position.

8. Respond to that objection (crediting any point in it that is worthy of concession).

Consider the following example: Note that in this example we use a reference to support our thesis.

1. **Find two important conflicting ideas.** The two ideas I will focus on for this example are the ideas of freedom versus law.

2. **Express an important problem that exists because of one conflict between the ideas you have selected.** There is often a conflict between the freedoms people should be allowed and the laws that are passed to protect people who might misuse their freedoms.

3. **Decide on an important point you want to make about that idea. This is your thesis.** It is my belief that the laws and the administration of those laws should allow for the maximum possible individual freedoms, and that all laws that deny people their basic rights should be revoked.

4. **Elaborate your thesis.** In the United States, at present, there seem to be a growing number of laws that deny people some fundamental human right or other. More and more behavior is being criminalized. More and more people are going to prison for acts that don't harm other people. In many cases the law — penalizing acts that are merely socially disapproved of — are themselves unethical.

5. **Exemplify your thesis.** Consider, for example, the many laws governing consensual adult behaviors. In his book entitled, *Ain't Nobody's Business if You Do*, Peter McWilliams (1996) says: "More than 750,000 people are in jail *right now* because of something they did that did not physically harm the person or property of another. In addition, more than 3,000,000 people are on parole or probation for consensual crimes. Further, more than 4,000,000 people are arrested each year for doing something that hurts no one but, potentially, themselves." Among McWilliams' list of the most popular consensual crimes are: "gambling, recreational drug use, religious and psychologically therapeutic drug use, prostitution, pornography and obscenity, violations of marriage (adultery, fornication, cohabitation, sodomy, bigamy, polygamy), homosexuality, regenerative drug use, unorthodox medical practices ("Quacks!"), unconventional religious practices ("Cults!"), unpopular political views ("Commies!"), suicide and assisted suicide, transvestism, not using safety devices (such as motorcycle helmets and seat belts), public drunkenness, jaywalking, and loitering and vagrancy (as long as they don't become trespassing or disturbing the peace)." In short, I agree with McWilliams when he says, "You should be allowed to do whatever you want with your own person and property, as long as you don't physically harm the person or property of a non-consenting other."

6. **Illustrate your thesis.** To illustrate, consider public nudity, which is against the law. For most people it is upsetting to imagine humans walking around in public without clothes on. Such behavior is considered unethical, and has been made illegal. But imagine what the animal kingdom would look like if all animals, not just humans, were forced to clothe themselves, to keep their private parts covered. Imagine horses and dogs and cats wearing shorts and shirts. Consider

making it illegal for animals to go about living an animal life without clothes. The very idea is absurd. The fact is that we get upset if people are publicly nude but not if animals are nude. Yet, we too are animals. Human nudity is no more innately *disgusting* than any other animal nudity.

7. **Formulate at least one problem that a reasonable person (who thinks differently from you) might have with your position.** A reasonable person opposed to my viewpoint might argue that though many laws violate people's basic rights, legislators who make the laws in a democratic society are carrying out the views of the majority of the people, that the only way to change this in a democratic society is to educate people about the implications of unethical laws and hope that they will fight for more reasonable ones.

8. **Respond to that problem (crediting any point in the objection that is worthy of concession).** I agree that the only way a democracy can work well is when people are educated and therefore able to think through complex issues. I agree that the people are allowing legislators to speak for them, rather than speaking up for themselves, that people need to become involved in important issues and refuse to support over-zealous law-making. Nevertheless, I also think that the majority often is prone to think in a narrow sociocentric manner and therefore to inadvertently support the violation of human rights. I think that the U.S. Bill of Rights should be expanded to encompass the whole of the U.N. Declaration of Human Rights, and that through education we move toward living in accordance with both of these documents.

Exploring Key Ideas Within Disciplines

In this section we present you with two exercises focusing on key ideas in a number of disciplines. The ideas are significant both academically and in human life. In some cases we ask you to focus on the very idea of the discipline itself. By stating, elaborating, exemplifying, and illustrating the ideas, you will find yourself engaged in substantive writing about each of the disciplines you target.

For example, consider answering the following questions, as part of the process of learning to think biologically:

- Could you state what photosynthesis is in one simple sentence?
- Could you elaborate more fully what is involved in photosynthesis?
- Could you give me an example of photosynthesis?
- Could you give me an analogy or metaphor to help me see what photosynthesis is like?

The same four questions can be formulated for explaining a democracy, an equation, mass, energy, a chemical reaction, the key problem facing the main character in a story, the main point in a story, and indeed any important concept whatever. Every subject area has a network or system of concepts that must be internalized to think successfully within the subject. When we can answer these four questions for fundamental concepts within disciplines, we begin to take command of both the concepts and the disciplines.

Exercise # 1

We now can suggest a practice pattern for any concept, say "X."

X is best defined as _____

In other words, _____

For example, _____

To illustrate my explanation with an analogy, X is like _____

Practice writing your understanding of five key concepts within disciplines, using the format above. Here are some key ideas you might consider: Science, Chemistry, Biology, Botany, Geology, Ecology, Anthropology, Sociology, History, Economics, Politics, Psychology, Ethics, Theology, Literature, Philosophy, Painting, Sculpture, Music, Engineering, Logic, Mathematics, Physics. We suggest that you use relevant encyclopedias or other reference materials (e.g., textbooks) to figure out the meanings of these key concepts. But always write the meanings in your own words.

Once you have written your understanding of each concept, assess your writing by re-reading the explanation of the concept (from the relevant section in a textbook or other resource). By carefully comparing what you said (and didn't say) with the explanation in the textbook, you can identify strengths and weaknesses in your initial understanding of the concept.

Because every discipline contains key concepts or organizing ideas that guide everything else within the discipline, it is important to learn how to write in ways that help us internalize those concepts. Key concepts enable us to grasp the big picture of a discipline. We should master these concepts before learning subordinate concepts. In this section we provide examples of writing exercises that will enable you to "open up" key concepts in a discipline. The following exercise builds on the previous one.

Exercise # 2

Use the following guides for capturing the essence of key concepts:

1. State the meaning of the concept in one simple sentence.

2. State the significance of the idea to the discipline (in other words).

3. Give an example of the concept (as it applies to real life).

4. Give an analogy or metaphor of the concept to link the concept to similar ideas in other domains.

5. Connect the idea to other important ideas within the same domain of thought.

6. Give examples for item 5.

Here is a pattern for practicing the guidelines above:

1. X is...

2. In other words...

3. For example...

4. To illustrate my explanation with an analogy, X is like...

5. This idea is connected to the following ideas within the discipline...

6. Some examples that show the relationship between this idea and other important ideas are...

Example # 1 (focusing on history):

1. **State the meaning of the concept in one simple sentence.**
   History is the development of "stories" or accounts of the past with the purpose of understanding how and why things happened, and how we can use that understanding to live better in the present and future.

2. **State the significance of the idea to the discipline.**
   Understanding the concept of history is vital to one's ability

to think historically, to think like a historian. When we think about the nature of historical thinking, we discover that it is, by necessity, highly selective. For example, during any given historical period, even one as short as a day, millions of events take place, forcing those who would give an account of "yesterday" to leave out most of what actually happened. No given written history contains anything more than a tiny percentage of the total events that took place within the studied historical period. Historians therefore must regularly make value judgments to decide what to include and exclude from their accounts. The result is that there are different possible stories and accounts that highlight different patterns in the events themselves. One historian focuses on great and influential politicians and military figures, another on great ideas and artists, another on technology and its development, another on the role of economics, and another tries to say a little about each of these historical points of view. Because history is always told from some perspective, and every perspective is not equally sound, historical accounts are not necessarily of the same quality. Some historical accounts more accurately represent past events and provide more reasonable interpretations of those events.

3. **Give an example of the concept (as it applies to real life).** To think historically is to begin to connect history to everyday life. For example, all humans *create* their own story in the privacy of their minds. This is a form of historical thinking. By recognizing this, we can begin to analyze how we tell the story of our life. We can seek to determine the extent to which we accurately portray events in our past by listening to the historical accounts of our lives given by others. We might find that we are avoiding the truth about some part of our behavior. We might learn from the perspectives of others.

4. **Give an analogy or metaphor of the concept to link the concept to similar ideas in other domains.** We might compare history to novels. Just as history focuses on giving an account of the past, all novels are set in some time and place and give some account of what it was to live at that time in that place. Mark Twain's *Huckleberry Finn* gives us an account of life along the Mississippi River in the nineteenth century. Charles Dickens' *A Christmas Carol* gives us an account of what life was like for the rich and poor in London in the mid-nineteenth century.

John Steinbeck's *The Grapes of Wrath* gives us an account of the social dislocation of poor farmers (and of the indifference of large industry to private suffering) in the American states suffering from drought in the 1930s. Both history and novels usually include the character, decisions, and actions of people. Implications of decisions and/or events are usually highlighted in both.

5. **Connect the idea to other important ideas within the same domain of thought.** The idea of history is related to the ideas of *time, change, growth, progress, conflict, revolution, evolution, permanence, sociocentrism, social conventions, vested interest,* and *power.* To understand history, one must understand how it is connected to the human search to find meaning in life. The past is the key to the present and the future. In it we can find success and failure, waste and war, triumph and suffering, the beginnings of things, their growth and transformations, and their endings.

6. **Give examples.** History reveals short-term and long-term patterns. In history we find civilizations that last a hundred or thousands of years. We see the omnipresence of war and suffering. We see the powerful nations dominating the weak nations. We see some groups of people (the technologically advanced) virtually eliminating other groups — as in the domination of European peoples in conquering the Americas.

Example # 2 (focusing on biology):

1. **State the meaning of the concept in one simple sentence.** Biology is the scientific study of all life forms. Its basic goal is to understand how life forms work, including the fundamental processes and ingredients of all life forms.

2. **State the significance of the idea to the discipline.** Once one understands the basic idea of a life form, one is ready to understand the common denominators between the 10 million species of living things that exist in the world today. For example, all life forms, no matter how diverse, have the following common characteristics: (1) they are made up of cells, enclosed by a membrane that maintains internal conditions different from their surroundings; (2) they contain DNA or RNA as the material that carries their master plan; and (3) they carry out a process, called metabolism, which

involves the conversion of different forms of energy through predictable chemical reactions.

3. **Give an example of the concept (as it applies to real life).** To think biologically is to see the world as divided into living and non-living matter. It is to see all living things as part of complicated ecosystems. Thinking biologically, you also see living things in terms of the concepts of structure and function. Wherever there is life, you look for it to be structured in specific ways, and you look for all structures to have a function in that living thing.

4. **Give an analogy or metaphor of the concept to link the concept to similar ideas in other domains.** The notion of living things existing in systems, both internal and external, is similar to the way in which non-living matter exists in physical systems. Looking for "systems" is a hallmark of all science, not just of biology. For example, all chemists see the world as made up of atoms that can cluster together in discoverable structural patterns. Furthermore, they see these patterns as making possible transformations of substances from one state to another. Take one kind of chemical substance and mix it with or expose it to another kind of chemical substance and you may get a chemical reaction resulting in one or more new chemical substances.

5. **Connect the idea to other important ideas within the same domain of thought.** The idea of life forms is connected with the ideas of the structures that exist at different levels of life (from the smallest to the largest); for example, life at the level of chemical *molecules*, at the level of *organelles*, at the level of *cell, tissue, organ, organism, population, ecological community,* and *biosphere.*

6. **Give examples.** Biologists can study the role of specific molecules in the structure of organelles, or the role of organelles in the structure of cells, or the role of cells in the structure of tissues, or the role of tissues in the structure of organs, or the role of organs in the structure of organisms, and so forth. Each level of life has a specific relationship to all the others. This multi-system nature makes possible the linking of all sciences together into a massive system of systems.

Now you should practice

Focus on any key concepts within a discipline (see page 40 for ideas) and use the pattern just modeled to write substantively about them. Use good dictionaries, encyclopedias, and/or textbooks as references. Remember, there is no one correct answer for what you are doing. The question is: Does writing about this key concept help you gain insight into important dimensions of the powerful ways of thinking that all disciplines and subjects make possible?

Analyzing Reasoning

Substantive writing can be used to understand an author's reasoning, to enter into the author's thinking. To think through the logic of an author's reasoning, complete the following statements in writing (see Appendix A for a fuller template):

- The author's *purpose* is…
- The main *question* the author addresses in the article is…
- The most important *information* the author uses in reasoning through the question is…
- The most important *inferences* or conclusions the author comes to are…
- The key *concepts* the author uses in his or her thinking in writing the article are…
- The *assumptions* underlying the author's reasoning are…
- The *implications* of the author's views (if people take them seriously) are…
- The *main point of view* presented in the article is…

We now provide two brief excerpts. Read each one, then, using the template in Appendix A, write the logic of the author's reasoning. After doing so, compare your written work to the sample analysis that follows each excerpt.

Writing Substantively to Analyze Reasoning: An Example

A sample analysis follows this brief article.

Is it Possible for the News Media to Reform?[1]

To provide their publics with non-biased writing, journalists around the world, would have to, first, enter empathically into world views to which they are not at present sympathetic. They would have to imagine writing for audiences that hold views antithetical to the ones they hold. They would have to develop insights into their own sociocentrism. They would have to do the things done by critical consumers of the news. The most significant problem is that, were they to do so, their readers would perceive their articles as "biased" and "slanted," as "propaganda." These reporters would be seen as irresponsible, as allowing their personal point of view to bias their journalistic writings. Imagine Israeli journalists writing articles that present the Palestinian point of view sympathetically. Imagine Pakistani journalists writing articles that present the Indian point of view sympathetically.

The most basic point is this: journalists do not determine the nature and demands of their job. They do not determine what their readers want or think or hate or fear. The nature and demands of their job are determined by the broader nature of societies themselves and the beliefs, values and world views of its members. It is human nature to see the world, in the first instance, in egocentric and sociocentric terms. Most people are not interested in having their minds broadened. They want their present beliefs and values extolled and confirmed. Like football fans, they want the home team to win, and when it wins to triumph gloriously. If they lose, they want to be told that the game wasn't important, or that the other side cheated, or that the officials were biased against them.

As long as the overwhelming mass of persons in the broader society are drawn to news articles that reinforce, and do not question, their fundamental views or passions, the economic imperatives will remain the same. The logic is parallel to that of reforming a nation's eating habits. As long as the mass of people want high fat processed foods, the market will sell high fat and processed foods to them. And as long as the mass of people want simplistic news articles that reinforce egocentric and sociocentric thinking, that present the world in sweeping terms of good and evil (with the reader's views and passions treated as good and those of the reader's conceived enemies as evil), the news media will generate such articles for them. The profit and ratings of news sources that routinely reinforce the passions and prejudices of their readers will continue to soar.

[1] Paul, R. and Elder, L. (2003). *The Miniature Guide for Conscientious Citizens on How to Detect Media Bias and Propaganda*. Dillon Beach, CA: Foundation for Critical Thinking.

Sample Analysis

The main <u>purpose</u> of this article is to show why the news media are not likely to alter their traditional practices of slanting the news in keeping with audience preconceptions.

The key <u>question</u> that the author is addressing is: "Why is it not possible for the news media to reform?"

The most important <u>information</u> in this article is:

1. information about how and why the news media currently operates:
   a. that the news media slant stories to fit the viewpoint of their audience. "Most people are not interested in having their views broadened… Like football fans they want the home team to win… The overwhelming mass of persons in the broader society are drawn to news articles that reinforce, and do not question, their fundamental views or passions."
   b. that the fundamental purpose of the mainstream news media is to make money. "As long as the mass of people want simplistic news articles…the news media will generate such articles for them. The profit and ratings of news sources that routinely reinforce the passions and prejudices of their readers will continue to soar."

2. information about how the news media would have to change to be more intellectually responsible:
   a. that the news media would have to actively enter differing world views "Imagine Israeli journalists writing articles that

present the Palestinian point of view sympathetically. Imagine Pakistani journalists writing articles that present the Indian point of view sympathetically."

    b. that the news media would have to "develop insights into their own sociocentrism."

The main inferences in this article are: "As long as the overwhelming mass of persons in the broader society are drawn to news articles that reinforce, and do not question, their fundamental views or passions," the news will be presented in a biased way. Because the fundamental purpose of the media is to make money, and the only way people will buy papers is if their sociocentric views are reinforced and not questioned, the media will continue distort events in accordance with audience views.

The key concepts that guide the author's reasoning in this article are: biased and unbiased journalism, egocentrism and sociocentrism, propaganda. (Each of these concepts should be elaborated.)

The main assumptions underlying the author's thinking are: The driving force behind the news media is vested interest — i.e., making money; that the news media therefore pander to their readers' views so as to sell more papers; but that, at the same time, the news media must appear to function objectively and fairly.

If this line of reasoning is justified, the implications are: Citizens need to think critically about the news media and how they systematically distort stories in accordance with reader bias. People need to notice how their own sociocentric views are intensified by what they read.

The main point of view presented in this article is: The world news media function as profit-making enterprises that structure the news to pander to reader and society prejudices.

On the next three pages you will find another sample article analyzed (using the analysis template in Appendix A).

The Problem of Pseudo-Ethics
The Sociocentric Counterfeits of Ethical Reasoning[2]

Skilled ethical thinkers routinely distinguish ethics from other domains of thinking such as those of social conventions (conventional thinking), religion (theological thinking), politics (ideological thinking), and the law (legal thinking). Too often, ethics is confused with these very different modes of thinking. It is not uncommon, for example, for highly variant and conflicting social values and taboos to be treated as if they were universal ethical principles.

Thus, religious ideologies, social "rules," and laws are often mistakenly taken to be inherently ethical in nature. If we were to accept this amalgamation of domains, by implication every practice within any religious system would necessarily be ethical, every social rule ethically obligatory, and every law ethically justified.

If religion were to define ethics, we could not then judge any religious practices — e.g., torturing unbelievers or burning them alive — as unethical. In the same way, if ethical and conventional thinking were one and the same, every social practice within any culture would necessarily be ethically obligatory — including social conventions in Nazi Germany. We could not, then, condemn any social traditions, norms, mores, and taboos from an ethical standpoint — however ethically bankrupt they were. What's more, if the law were to define ethics, by implication politicians and lawyers would be considered experts on ethics and every law they finagled to get on the books would take on the status of a moral truth.

It is essential, then, to differentiate ethics from other modes of thinking commonly confused with ethics. We must remain free to critique commonly accepted social conventions, religious practices, political ideas, and laws, using ethical concepts not defined by them. No one lacking this ability can become proficient in ethical reasoning.

Examples of confusing ethical principles with theological beliefs:

- Members of majority religious groups sometimes enforce their beliefs on minorities.
- Members of religious groups sometimes act as if their theological beliefs are self-evidently true, scorning those who hold other views.
- Members of religious groups sometimes fail to recognize that "sin" is a theological concept, not an ethical one. ("Sin" is theologically defined.)
- Divergent religions do not agree on what is sinful (but

often expect their views to be enforced on all others as if a matter of universal ethics).

Examples of confusion between ethics and social conventions:

- Many societies have created taboos against showing various parts of the body and have severely punished those who violated the taboos.
- Many societies have created taboos against giving women the same rights as men.
- Many societies have socially legitimized religious persecution.
- Many societies have socially stigmatized interracial marriages.

Examples of confusing ethics and the law:

- Many sexual practices (such as homosexuality) have been unjustly punished with life imprisonment or death (under the laws of one society or another).
- Many societies have enforced unjust laws based on racist views.
- Many societies have enforced laws that discriminated against women.
- Many societies have enforced laws that discriminated against children.
- Many societies have made torture and/or slavery legal.
- Many societies have enforced laws arbitrarily punishing people for using some drugs but not others.

---

[2] Elder, L. and Paul, R. (2003). *The Miniature Guide to the Foundations of Analytic Thinking*. Dillon Beach, CA: Foundation for Critical Thinking.

Sample Analysis

The main purpose of this article is to convince the reader that ethics should not be confused with other modes of thinking — specifically religion, social conventions, and the law.

The key question that the author is addressing is: How does ethics differ from other ways of thinking?

The most important information in this article consists of:

1. Examples of confusing ethical principles with theological beliefs:

Members of majority religious groups often enforce their beliefs on minorities.

2. Examples of confusion between ethics and social conventions: Many societies have created taboos against showing various parts of the body and have severely punished those who violated the taboos.

3. Examples of confusing ethics and the law: Many sexual practices (such as homosexuality) have been unjustly punished with life imprisonment or death (under the laws of one society or another).

The main <u>inferences</u>/conclusions in this article are: that "it is essential to differentiate ethics from other modes of thinking commonly confused with ethics," and that only when we can differentiate ethics from other modes of thinking can we critique practices within other modes of thinking from an ethical perspective.

The key <u>ideas</u> that guide the author's reasoning in this article are: ethical reasoning, social conventions (conventional thinking), religion (theological thinking), politics (ideological thinking), and the law (legal thinking).

The main <u>assumptions</u> underlying the author's thinking are: that it is important for people to understand that ethics cannot be commandeered by or confused with other modes of thinking, that many people do not understand ethics as separate from other modes of reasoning, and that it is dangerous for people to consider ethics as something that can be defined by theology, society, or laws.

If this line of reasoning is justified, the <u>implications</u> are: that people need to understand ethics and to clearly separate in their own minds ethics from other modes of thinking often confused with ethics. Moreover, people need to call into question the common practice of confusing ethics with other domains of thought. If they fail to do so, religious practices, social conventions, and the law will determine what is to be considered ethical within a society.

The main <u>point of view</u> presented in this article is: that people largely fail to differentiate ethics from other modes of thinking, and, therefore, they often use the wrong standards for determining what is ethically right and wrong in human conduct.

Evaluating Reasoning

Every written piece is not of the same quality. We can assess what we write by applying intellectual standards to it — standards such as clarity, precision, accuracy, relevance, significant, depth, breadth, logic, and fairness. We might be clear in stating our position, while at the same time using information that is not accurate. We might use relevant information in a written piece but fail to think through the complexities of the issue (e.g., fail to achieve depth). Our argument might be logical but not significant. As writers, then, we need to become adept at assessing the quality of our reasoning.

To assess our writing, we should ask the following questions:

(1) Is our meaning **clearly** stated (or is our writing vague, confused, or muddled in some way)?

(2) Have we been **accurate** in what we have claimed?

(3) Have we been sufficiently **precise** in providing details and specifics (when specifics are relevant)?

(4) Do we stray from our purpose (thereby introducing **irrelevant** material)?

(5) Do we take the reader into the important complexities inherent in the subject (or is our writing **superficial**)?

(6) Is our writing overly **narrow** in its perspective?

(7) Is our writing internally consistent (or are there unexplained **contradictions** in the text)?

(8) Have we said something **significant** (or have we dealt with the subject in a trivial manner)?

(9) Have we been **fair** (or have we taken a one-sided, narrow approach)?

It's your turn to practice

Use the template in Appendix B to assess the logic of the author's reasoning in the previous two examples (the *Analyzing Reasoning* section).

References

Frankl, Viktor E. (1959). *Man's Search for Meaning*. NY, NY: Washington Square Press.
McWilliams, Peter. (1996). *Ain't Nobody's Business If You Do: The Absurdity of Consensual Crimes in Our Free Country*. Los Angeles, CA: Prelude Press, pp. 3, 7.
Mencken, H. L. (1922). *Prejudices*, Third Series. NY, NY: Octagon Books.
Myers, Gustavus. (1907). *History of the Great American Fortunes*. Chicago, IL: Charles H. Kerr & Co.

Appendix A: The Logic of an Article

One important way to understand an essay, article, or chapter is through the analysis of the parts of the author's reasoning. Once you have done this, you can evaluate the author's reasoning using intellectual standards. Here is a template to follow:

(1) The main **purpose** of this article is _____.
(Here you are trying to state, as accurately as possible, the author's intent in writing the article. What was the author trying to accomplish?)

(2) The key **question** that the author is addressing is _____. (Your goal is to figure out the key question that was in the mind of the author when he/she wrote the article. What was the key question addressed in the article?)

(3) The most important **information** in this article is _____.
(You want to identify the key information the author used, or presupposed, in the article to support his/her main arguments. Here you are looking for facts, experiences, and/or data the author is using to support his/her conclusions.)

(4) The main **inferences** in this article are _____
_____.
(You want to identify the most important conclusions the author comes to and presents in the article.)

(5) The key **concept**(s) we need to understand in this article is (are)_____. By these concepts the author means_____.
(To identify these ideas, ask yourself: What are the most important ideas that you would have to know to understand the author's line of reasoning? Then briefly elaborate what the author means by these ideas.)

(6) The main **assumption**(s) underlying the author's thinking is (are)_____. (Ask yourself: What is the author taking for granted [that might be questioned]? The assumptions are generalizations that the author does not think he/she has to defend in the context of writing the article, and they are usually unstated. This is where the author's thinking logically begins.)

(7a) If we take this line of reasoning seriously, the **implications** are

_____.

(What consequences are likely to follow if people take the author's line of reasoning seriously? Here you are to pursue the logical implications of the author's position. You should include implications that the author states, and also those that the author does not state.)

(7b) If we fail to take this line of reasoning seriously, the **implications** are _____.
(What consequences are likely to follow if people ignore the author's reasoning?)

(8) The main **point(s) of view** presented in this article is (are)

_____.

(The main question you are trying to answer here is: What is the author looking at, and how is he/she seeing it? For example, in this guide we are looking at "writing" and seeing it "as requiring intellectual discipline and routine practice.")

If you truly understand these structures as they interrelate in an article, essay, or chapter, you should be able to empathically role-play the thinking of the author. These are the eight basic structures that define all reasoning. They are the essential elements of thought.

Appendix B:
Evaluating an Author's Reasoning

1. Identify the author's **purpose:** Is the purpose of the author well-stated or clearly implied? Is it justifiable?

2. Identify the key **question** which the written piece answers: Is the question at issue well-stated (or clearly implied)? Is it clear and unbiased? Does the expression of the question do justice to the complexity of the matter at issue? Are the question and purpose directly relevant to each other?

3. Identify the most important **information** presented by the author: Does the writer cite relevant evidence, experiences, and/or information essential to the issue? Is the information accurate and directly relevant to the question at issue? Does the writer address the complexities of the issue?

4. Identify the most fundamental **concepts** which are at the heart of the author's reasoning: Does the writer clarify key ideas when necessary? Are the ideas used justifiably?

5. Identify the author's **assumptions:** Does the writer show a sensitivity to what he or she is taking for granted or assuming (insofar as those assumptions might reasonably be questioned)? Or does the writer use questionable assumptions without addressing problems inherent in those assumptions?

6. Identify the most important **inferences** or conclusions in the written piece: Do the inferences and conclusions made by the author clearly follow from the information relevant to the issue, or does the author jump to unjustifiable conclusions? Does the author consider alternative conclusions where the issue is complex? In other words, does the author use a sound line of reasoning to come to logical conclusions, or can you identify flaws in the reasoning somewhere?

7. Identify the author's **point of view:** Does the author show a sensitivity to alternative relevant points of view or lines of reasoning? Does he or she consider and respond to objections framed from other relevant points of view?

8. Identify **implications:** Does the writer display a sensitivity to the implications and consequences of the position he or she is taking?

Appendix C

For Instructors

Mapping Sentences

The English language has five basic sentence patterns that every student should be able to recognize. These sentences consist of one or more clauses and are constructed as shown below.

There are two kinds of clauses in English: independent (I) and dependent (D), as follows:

I ⟶ **subject + predicate** (Jack went to the library)

D ⟶ **subordinator + I** (since Jack went to the library)

There are three kinds of connectors: coordinators, subordinators, and transitional words.

There are only six **coordinators**: and, or, nor, but, yet, for.

There are many **subordinators**, including, among others: because, if, since, even though. Placed in front of an independent clause, a subordinator makes it dependent.

There are many **transitional words**, among them: however, therefore, nevertheless, of course. (See a map of transitional words and their functions on page 59.)

Five major English sentence patterns:

(1) **I** (Jack went to the library.)

(2) **I, coordinator I** (Jack went to the library, and Frank went with him.)

(3) **I D** (Jack went to the library because he wanted to check out a book.)

(4) **D, I** (Because he wanted to check out a book, Jack went to the library.)

(5) **I; transitional word, I** (Jack went to the library; however, the book he wanted was checked out.)

Appendix D

For Instructors

How to Teach Students to Assess Writing

Writing is a powerful tool in learning. Yet, many instructors avoid assigning writing to avoid excessive grading. Actually, it is possible to develop writing-intensive classes within all disciplines without having to grade lots of papers. This can be accomplished by: (a) having students maintain a portfolio of their work, (b) regularly requiring students to bring their written work to class, (c) using the activities below as means of providing students with high-quality peer-feedback, (d) modeling before the class the feedback you want students to give (use the guidelines for assessing reasoning in Appendix B), and (e) grading the work in the portfolio periodically and randomly — for example, grading one paper in seven. The result is that students get individualized daily feedback from peers. The instructor gives daily feedback to the class as a whole, but only periodic and selective feedback to individual students.

<u>First Strategy</u>. Begin with a brief review of the criteria to be used in giving feedback. Working in groups of three or four, students take turns reading their papers aloud slowly and discussing the extent to which they have or have not fulfilled the performance criteria relevant to the paper. All recommendations must be constructive, indicating where and how each paper could be improved.

<u>Second Strategy</u>. Begin with a brief review of the criteria to be used in giving feedback. Working in groups of four, students choose the best paper (using standards of clarity, logic, etc. as well as any specific criteria you have given them). Then they join with a second group and choose the best paper of the two (one from each group). These papers (chosen by the eight-person groups) are collected and read

to the class as a whole. A class-wide discussion is held, under your direction, to make clear the strengths and weaknesses of the competing remaining papers, leading to the class voting on the best paper of the day (again, using explicit intellectual standards in the assessment).

Third Strategy. Begin with a brief review of the criteria to be used in giving feedback. Working in groups of three or four, students write out their recommendations for improvement on three or four papers (from students not in the group). All recommendations must be constructive, indicating where and how each paper could be improved. The written recommendations go back to the original writers, who do a revised draft for the next class. Using this method, all students receive written feedback on their papers from a "team" of critics using specific guidelines.

Fourth Strategy. Begin with a brief review of the criteria to be used in giving feedback. One student's paper is read aloud slowly to the class while the instructor leads a class-wide discussion on how the paper might be improved. All recommendations must be constructive, indicating where and how each paper could be improved. This discussion serves as a model for what is expected in the assessment process. Then the students work in groups of two or three to try to come up with recommendations for improvement for the students in their group (based on the model established by the instructor).

Students write regularly to internalize the skills and knowledge required in the discipline, learning at the same time how to assess and improve their work. The instructor serves as a model, leader, and supervisor, but is not burdened by extensive grading of papers.

Appendix E:

The Function of Transitional Words

Connectives	How they are used	Examples
besides what's more furthermore in addition	To add another thought	Two postal cards are often more effective than one letter. *Besides,* they are cheaper.
for example for instance in other words	To add an example	He has lost confidence in his game. *For example,* yesterday he got nervous at the end of the match.
in fact as a matter of fact	To add emphasis to an idea	Last week I was ill, *in fact,* I had to stay in bed until Monday.
therefore consequently	To highlight what follows	The President vetoed the bill. *Consequently,* it never became a law.
of course to be sure though still however on the other hand nevertheless rather	To grant an exception	He said he would study all day. I doubt it, *though.* I like to paint; *however,* I can't understand modern art.
first next finally meanwhile later afterwards nearby eventually above beyond	To arrange ideas in order, time, or space	*First,* drink some fruit juice. *Next,* have a bowl of soup. *Then* eat the quiche. *Finally,* have some pie and coffee.
in short in brief to sum up in summary in conclusion	To sum up several ideas	Scientists say that we should eat food that has all the proteins, fats, and vitamins we need. *In short,* they recommend a balanced diet.

The Thinker's Guide Series

The Thinker's Guide series provides convenient, inexpensive, portable references that students and faculty can use to improve the quality of studying, learning, and teaching. Their modest cost enables instructors to require them of all students (in addition to a textbook). Their compactness enables students to keep them at hand whenever they are working in or out of class. Their succinctness serves as a continual reminder of the most basic principles of critical thinking.

For Students & Faculty

How to Read a Paragraph
This guide provides theory and activities necessary for deep comprehension. Imminently practical for students. (1-24 copies $6.00 each; 25-199 copies $4.00 each; 200-499 copies $2.50 each)

Critical Thinking
The essence of critical thinking concepts and tools distilled into a 19-page pocket-size guide. (1-24 copies $4.00 each; 25-199 copies $2.00 each; 200-499 copies $1.75 each)

How to Study & Learn
A variety of strategies—both simple and complex—for becoming not just a better student, but also a master student. (1-24 copies $6.00 each; 25-199 copies $4.00 each; 200-499 copies $2.50 each)

Analytic Thinking
This guide focuses on the intellectual skills that enable one to analyze anything one might think about — questions, problems, disciplines, subjects, etc. It provides the common denominator between all forms of analysis. (1-24 copies $6.00 each; 25-199 copies $4.00 each; 200-499 copies $2.50 each)

Scientific Thinking
The essence of scientific thinking concepts and tools. It focuses on the intellectual skills inherent in the well-cultivated scientific thinker. (1-24 copies $6.00 each; 25-199 copies $4.00 each; 200-499 copies $2.50 each)

The Human Mind
Designed to give the reader insight into the basic functions of the human mind and to how knowledge of these functions (and their interrelations) can enable one to use one's intellect and emotions more effectively (1-24 copies $5.00 each; 25-199 copies $2.50 each; 200-499 copies $1.75 each)

How to Detect Media Bias and Propaganda
Designed to help readers come to recognize bias in their nation's news, to detect ideology, slant, and spin at work, and to recognize propaganda when exposed to it, so that they can reasonably determine what media messages need to be supplemented, counter-balanced or thrown out entirely. It focuses on the internal logic of the news as well as societal influences on the media. (1-24 copies $5.00 each; 25-199 copies $2.50 each; 200-499 copies $1.75 each)

Asking Essential Questions
Introduces the art of asking essential questions. It is best used in conjunction with the **Miniature Guide to Critical Thinking** and the **How to Study** mini-guide. (1-24 copies $6.00 each; 25-199 copies $4.00 each; 200-499 copies $2.50 each)

Foundations of Ethical Reasoning
Provides insights into the nature of ethical reasoning, why it is so often flawed, and how to avoid those flaws. It lays out the function of ethics, its main impediments, and its social counterfeits. (1-24 copies $6.00 each; 25-199 copies $4.00 each; 200-499 copies $2.50 each)

Critical Thinking for Children
Designed for K-6 classroom use. Focuses on explaining basic critical thinking principles to young children using cartoon characters. (1-24 copies $5.00 each; 25-199 copies $2.50 each; 200-499 copies $1.75 each)

For Faculty

Active and Cooperative Learning
Provides 27 simple ideas for the improvement of instruction. It lays the foundation for the ideas found in the mini-guide **How to Improve Student Learning**. (1-24 copies $3.00 each; 25-199 copies $1.50 each; 200-499 copies $1.25 each)

How to Improve Student Learning
Provides 30 practical ideas for the improvement of instruction based on critical thinking concepts and tools. It builds on, and goes beyond, the ideas in the mini-guide **Active and Cooperative Learning**. It cultivates student learning encouraged in the **How to Study and Learn** mini-guide. (1-24 copies $6.00 each; 25-199 copies $4.00 each; 200-499 copies $2.50 each)